WHSmith

Revision

English

Louis Fidge

Age 6–7
Year 2
Key Stage 1

The WHS Revision series

The *WHS Revision* books enable you to help your child revise and practise important skills taught in school. These skills form part of the National Curriculum and will help your child to improve his or her Maths and English.

Testing in schools

During their time at school all children will undergo a variety of tests. Regular testing is a feature of all schools. It is carried out:

● *informally* – in everyday classroom activities your child's teacher is continually assessing and observing your child's performance in a general way
● *formally* – more regular formal testing helps the teacher check your child's progress in specific areas.

Testing is important because:

● it provides evidence of your child's achievement and progress
● it helps the teacher decide which skills to focus on with your child
● it helps compare how different children are progressing.

The importance of revision

Regular revision is important to ensure your child remembers and practises skills he or she has been taught. These books will help your child revise and test his or her knowledge of some of the things he or she will be expected to know. They will help you prepare your child to be in a better position to face tests in school with confidence.

How to use this book

Units

This book is divided into forty units. Each unit begins with a **Remember** section, which introduces and revises essential information about the particular skill covered. If possible, read and discuss this with your child to ensure he or she understands it.

This is followed by a **Have a go** section, which contains a number of activities to help your child revise the topic thoroughly and use the skill effectively. Usually, your child should be able to undertake these activities fairly independently.

Revision tests

There are four revision tests in this book (pages 44–51). These test the skills covered in the preceding units and assess your child's progress and understanding. They can be marked by you or by your child. Your child should fill in his or her test score for each test in the space provided. This will provide a visual record of your child's progress and an instant sense of confidence and achievement.

Parents' notes

The parents' notes (on pages 52–55) provide you with brief information on each skill and explain why it is important.

Answers

Answers to the unit questions and tests may be found on pages 56–64.

Hachette UK's policy is to use papers that are natural, renewable and recyclable products and made from wood grown in sustainable forests. The logging and manufacturing processes are expected to conform to the environmental regulations of the country of origin.

Orders: please contact Bookpoint Ltd, 130 Milton Park, Abingdon, Oxon OX14 4SB. Telephone: (44) 01235 827720. Fax: (44) 01235 400454. Lines are open 9.00a.m.–5.00p.m., Monday to Saturday, with a 24-hour message answering service. Visit our website at www. hoddereducation.co.uk.

© Louis Fidge 2013
First published in 2007 exclusively for WHSmith by
Hodder Education
An Hachette UK Company
338 Euston Road
London NW1 3BH

This second edition first published in 2013 exclusively for WHSmith by Hodder Education.

Impression number   10 9 8 7 6 5 4 3 2
Year   2018 2017 2016 2015 2014

This edition has been updated, 2014, to reflect National Curriculum changes.

Cover illustration by Oxford Designers and Illustrators Ltd
All other illustrations by Fakenham Prepress Solutions, Fakenham, Norfolk NR21 8NN
Typeset in 16pt Folio by Fakenham Prepress Solutions, Fakenham, Norfolk NR21 8NN
Printed in Italy

A catalogue record for this title is available from the British Library.

ISBN: 978 1444 188 271

Contents

Unit 1: Vowels and consonants (1)

◯ Remember

There are **five vowels** in the alphabet. They are **a, e, i, o** and **u**.

All the other letters are **consonants**.

Most words have **at least one vowel**.

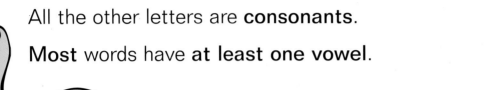

a b c d e f g h i j k l m n o p q r s t u v w x y z

◯ Have a go

1 Read the words. Underline the vowel in each word.

hat	bed	pin	cot	but
sip	fat	sun	get	pot
hug	net	lap	fog	bin

2 Put in the missing vowel in each word.

a	b	c	d	e
fr_o_g	dr_u_m	s_a_ck	l_e_g	k_i_ss

f	g	h	i	j
r__g	h_i_ll	n_e_st	m_a_p	b_a_g

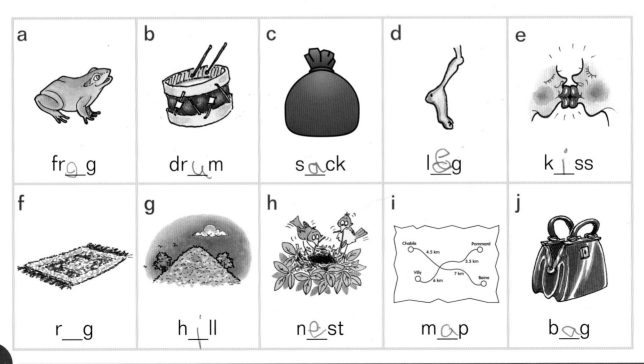

4

Unit 2: Vowels and consonants (2)

⬤ Remember

Look at the 26 letters in the alphabet below.
A, e, i, o and u are **vowels**.
The other letters are **consonants**

a b c d **e** f g h **i** j k l m n **o** p q r s t **u** v w x y z

⬤ Have a go

1 Choose the correct vowel to complete each word.

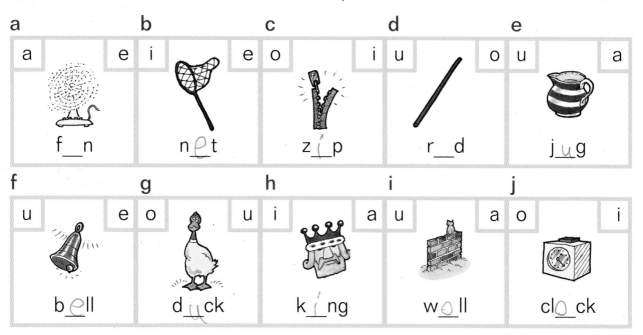

a	b	c	d	e
a · e	i · e o	· i u	o u · a	
f _ n	n _e_ t	z _i_ p	r _ d	j _u_ g

f	g	h	i	j
u · e o	· u i	· a u	a o · i	
b _e_ ll	d _u_ ck	k _i_ ng	w _o_ ll	cl _o_ ck

2 Fill in the two missing vowels in each word.

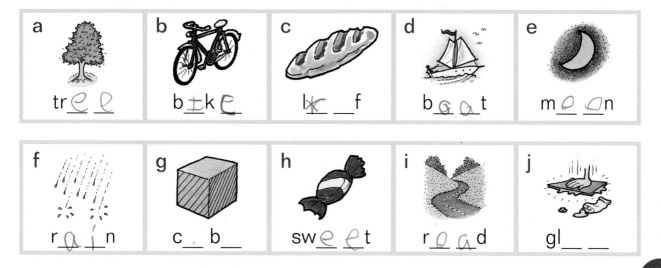

a	b	c	d	e
tr _e_ _e_	b _i_ k _e_	l _ f	b _o_ _a_ t	m _o_ _o_ n

f	g	h	i	j
r _a_ _i_ n	c _ b _ _	sw _e_ _e_ t	r _o_ _a_ d	gl _ _ _

Remember

When we spell words we have to build them up from **phonemes** (**letters** or **groups of letters**).

c + a + t

cat

d + o + g

dog

Have a go

1 Do these word sums. One is done for you.

a m + a + p = __map__

b h + e + n = _hen_

c s + i + x = _six_

d c + o + t = _cat_

e h + u + t = _hut_

f z + i + p = _zip_

g p + e + g = _peg_

h c + a + p = _cap_

i l + o + g = _log_

j m + u + g = _mug_

2 Use the words you have made. Write the correct word under each picture.

a

b

c

d

e

f

g

h

i

j

⬤ Remember

Here are some more examples of words built from phonemes.
(**letters** and **groups of letters**).

c + l + a + p

f + i + sh

s + ea + t

⬤ Have a go

Join up the phonemes. Write the word.
Match up each word to the correct animal.

a f + r + o + g   frog

b d + ee + r   _deer_

c g + oa + t   _goat_

d r + a + t   _rat_

e ch + i + ck   _chick_

f s + n + ai + l   _snail_

g s + n + a + ke   _snake_

h d + u + ck   _duck_

i f + o + x   _fox_

j sh + ee + p   _sheep_

● Remember

We have to **listen** carefully to **hear** words that **rhyme**.

Sometimes rhyming words have the **same letters** at the **end**.

moon   spoon

● Have a go

Join up the pairs of rhyming words.

Write the words here.
Read the words.

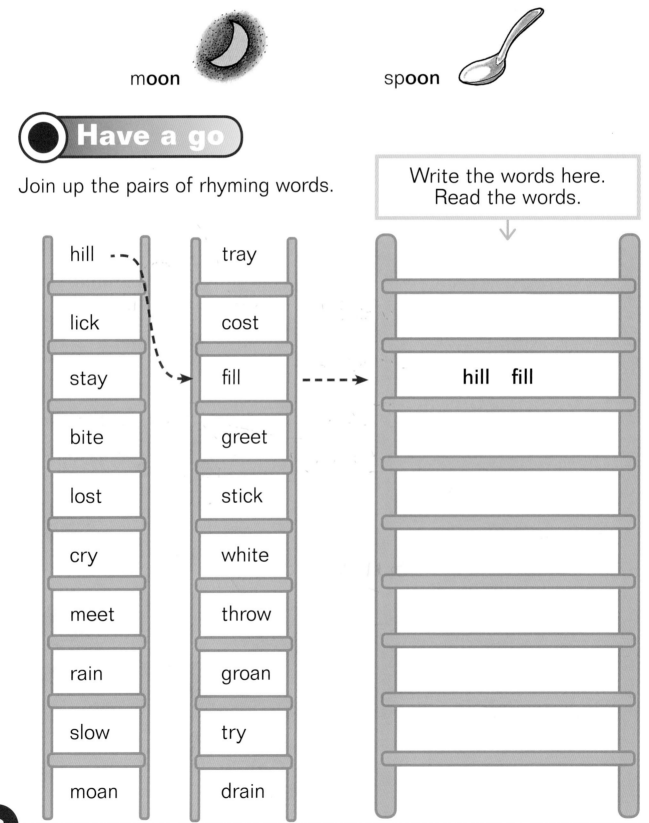

hill   tray

lick   cost

stay   fill

bite   greet

lost   stick

cry   white

meet   throw

rain   groan

slow   try

moan   drain

hill   fill

Unit 6: Rhyming (2)

● Remember

Here is a sentence with some words that **rhyme**.

The m**an** in the v**an** saw a fr**og** on a l**og**.

● Have a go

❶ Colour all the:

> **ight** words red   **ook** words blue
> **ound** words green   **ark** words yellow

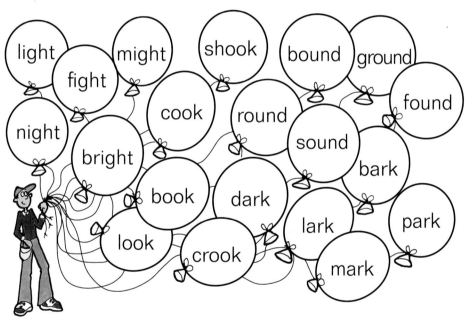

❷ Write the words here:

ight words	ook words	ound words	ark words

Remember

Every sentence must **make sense**.

The monkey ate a < bath.
banana.

The monkey ate a banana.

Have a go

Choose the best ending for each sentence. One has been done for you.

a A car has < four wheels.
four hands.

___A car has four wheels.___

b The mouse < roared.
squeaked.

_____

c Tom drank < an apple.
a cup of tea.

_____

d The girl read < the bus.
the book.

_____

e A squirrel ran < up the tree.
above the tree.

_____

f An apple has < lots of pips.
lots of pops.

_____

g The lion < roared.
reared.

_____

● Remember

A sentence should **make sense**.

The plane landed on ~~at~~ the runway.

plane
The /landed on the runway.

> This sentence has an **extra** word. It does **not make sense**.

> This sentence **does not make sense**. It has a word **missing**.

● Have a go

1 Write each sentence again.
Miss out the extra word that is not needed.

a The cat sat on the the mat. _____

b A house has a a roof. _____

c The boy read a some book. _____

d I fell into on the water. _____

e The girl lost her its bag. _____

f The plane flew landed in the sky. _____

2 Think of a sensible word to fill each gap.

a An ice cream is _____.

b A ball is _____.

c A lemon is _____.

d A baby cat is called a _____.

e You _____ a kettle.

f You _____ a nail with a hammer.

Unit 9: Capital letters and full stops

Every sentence must **begin** with a capital letter.

The horse is in a field.

Many sentences **end** with a **full stop**.

Write these sentences correctly. They make a story.

a claire ran home from school

_____

b she felt very hungry

_____

c claire went into the kitchen

_____

d she made some cheese sandwiches

_____

e then she put some cakes on the table

_____

f next claire put some crisps in a dish

_____

g after this she made a drink

_____

h when everything was ready claire had her tea

_____

 **Remember**

We put a **question mark** at the end of a **question**.

We put a **full stop** at the end of a **sentence**.

What is the matter?

I am lost.

 **Have a go**

Write these sentences and questions correctly.

a when is your birthday   it is in September

_____   _____

b where do you live   i live in Bedford

_____   _____

c what do you like at school   i like reading best

_____   _____

d what is the capital of France   Paris is the capital of France

_____   _____

e which is the first month of   January is the first month
  the year

_____   _____

f in which month is Christmas   Christmas is in December

_____   _____

Unit 11: Checking up on nouns

⬤ Remember

Some words **name** things. They are called **nouns**, or **naming words**.

apple

fish

hill

⬤ Have a go

❶ Write the correct noun in each gap.

aeroplane   boat   fire engine   submarine   train   ambulance

a A _____ floats on water.

b An _____ takes sick people to hospital.

c An _____ flies in the sky.

d A _____ carries firefighters to a fire.

e A _____ is a ship that can travel underwater.

f A _____ runs on rails and carries people.

❷ Fill each gap with a suitable noun.

a Children are taught in a _____.

b A _____ is a tool for hitting things like nails.

c You turn on a _____ to get water.

d We need _____ to buy things.

e A _____ is used to cut food when we eat.

f You can see through a _____ because it is made of glass.

Unit 12: Nouns — *a* or *an*?

Remember

We use **an** in front of a noun that begins with a **vowel**.

an ambulance

We use **a** in front of a noun that begins with a **consonant**.

a bridge

Have a go

1 Write **a** or **an** in front of each noun.

a 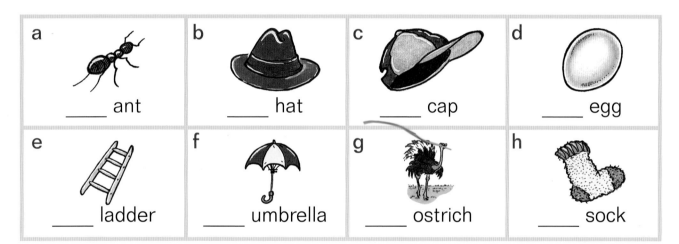 ____ ant	b ____ hat	c ____ cap	d ____ egg
e ____ ladder	f ____ umbrella	g ____ ostrich	h ____ sock

2 Choose **a** or **an** to fill each gap.

a   I saw ___ ostrich eating ___ orange.

b   Sam had ___ drink from ___ bottle.

c   You will need ___ umbrella in ___ rainstorm.

d   ___ child sat on ___ ant.

e   Will you buy me ___ comic from ___ shop?

f   There was ___ aeroplane on the runway at ___ airport.

Unit 13: Sentences

Sentences we write should **make sense**.
The beginning and ending of these sentences
have got mixed up.

Fish can ⟶ fly. ⟶ Birds can fly.

Birds can ⟶ swim. ⟶ Fish can swim.

Have a go

❶ Match up the beginning and ending of each sentence.

Write the sentences correctly.

Snakes	swim.	_____
Birds	gallop.	_____
Sharks	slither. ⟶	Snakes slither. _____
Butterflies	hop.	_____
Horses	fly.	_____
Frogs	flutter.	_____

❷ Match up the beginning and ending of each sentence.

Write each sentence and punctuate it correctly.

you drink	are very muddy	_____
the butterfly	flies in a rocket	_____
my shorts	a cup of tea	_____
you drive a car	like to eat bones	_____
an astronaut	fluttered its wings	_____
dogs	on the road	_____

Unit 14: Silly sentences

Some sentences sound very silly if we put some **words** in the **wrong order**!

The ball kicked the boy.   The boy kicked the ball.

1 Write these sentences again, so they make sense.
One has been done for you.

a   The egg ate the boy.   <u>The boy ate the egg.</u>

b   The cake cooked the lady.   _____

c   The car drove the man.   _____

d   The tree ran up the squirrel. _____

e   The fish ate the shark.   _____

f   The case picked up the girl. _____

g   The banana peeled a monkey. _____

h   The book read a teacher.   _____

2 Make up some silly sentences of your own like the ones above.

_____

_____

_____

_____

_____

_____

Remember

The letters **ar** often **come together** in words.
It is a common **letter pattern**.

a car

a card

Have a go

1 Add **ar** to the end of each word. Read the words you make.

a	b	c	d	e	f
<u>car</u> _____	b_____ _____	f_____ _____	j_____ _____	t_____ _____	st_____ _____

2 Read the words. Underline the **ar** in each word:

dark	harm	part	shark
charm	party	smart	farm
spark	bark	chart	alarm
park	cart	lark	dart

2 Write the words from question 2 in this chart:

arm words	**ark** words	**art** words

18

Unit 16: Letter patterns — *oi* and *oy*

● Remember

The letters **oy** and **oi** are common **letter patterns**.
They make the **same** sound.

boy

boil

| Remember that **oy** usually comes at the **end** of a word. | Remember that **oi** usually comes **inside** a word. |

● Have a go

① Make the words. Read the words you make.

a c + oi + l   b p + oi + n + t   c j + oy   d t + oy

_____   _____   _____   _____

② Use the words you made.
Write each word under the correct picture.

a   b   c   d

_____   _____   _____   _____

③ Complete the words in the boxes with **oy** or **oi**.
Use the words to complete the sentences.

| c___n | b___ | sp__l | ann___ | j___nt | enj___ |

a Tom is a kind _____ .

b The cook carved the _____ of meat.

c A penny is a type of _____ .

d I _____ reading and maths at school.

e I hate people who _____ me and _____ my games.

19

Unit 17: Compound words (1)

● Remember

Compound words are made up of **two smaller words joined together**.

pan

\+

cake

\=

pancake

● Have a go

① Do these word sums. Write the compound words you make.

a farm + yard = _____   **b** sea + side = _____

c bath + room = _____   **d** sheep + dog = _____

e sun + shine = _____   **f** snow + man = _____

g key + hole = _____   **h** run + way = _____

② Write the correct compound word under each picture.

a  _____	**b**  _____	**c**  _____	**d**  _____
e  _____	**f**  _____	**g**  _____	**h**  _____

Unit 18: Compound words (2)

⬤ Remember

A **compound word** is made when two smaller words are joined together.

farm + yard = farmyard

⬤ Have a go

Make some compound words.

Write the words here.

bed	ball
sun	brush
foot	room → bedroom
hand	fly
hair	case
wind	shine
butter	mill
book	bag
grand	way
motor	cloth
table	mother

Remember

Doing words are called **verbs**.
A **verb** tells us what someone or something is **doing**.

A snake **slithers** through the grass.

Have a go

1 Write the correct verb in each gap.

| comb | read | bang | sing | tie | eat |

a You _____ a book.

b You _____ a song.

c You _____ a knot.

d You _____ your hair.

e You _____ a sandwich.

f You _____ a drum.

2 Fill each gap with a suitable verb.

a You c _____ a ladder.

b You p _____ a picture.

c You r _____ a bike.

d You m _____ the grass.

e You c _____ a ball.

f You s _____ in a bed.

Unit 20: Revising verbs (2)

Remember

Sometimes a verb is made up of **two words**.

Mr Banks **is driving** a bus.

Have a go

1 Choose 'is' or 'are' to complete each sentence.

a The baby _____ crying.

b The cars _____ going too fast.

c The leaves _____ turning brown.

d A lion _____ prowling.

e Some mice _____ squeaking.

f An eagle _____ swooping down.

g Lots of horses _____ galloping past.

h A duck _____ waddling along.

2 Write each sentence again. Use two words for each verb.

a Mr Smith <u>washes</u> his car.   <u>Mr Smith is washing his car.</u>

b The teacher <u>helps</u> Sam. _____

c Beth <u>paints</u> a lovely picture. _____

d The cat <u>drinks</u> some milk. _____

e The lady <u>picks</u> up her bag. _____

f A farmer <u>works</u> on his farm. _____

Remember

Antonyms are words which mean the **opposite**.

hot

cold

Have a go

Match up the pairs of opposites.

Write the words here.

fast	happy
hot	far
sad	slow
open	quiet
noisy	cold
near	shut
weak	dry
heavy	strong
fat	short
long	thin
wet	light

_____

_____

fast   slow

_____

_____

_____

_____

_____

_____

_____

Remember

Words which mean the **opposite** are called **antonyms**.

sweet

sour

Have a go

1 Choose the best word to complete each sentence.

| sour | huge | long | cold | soft | dark |

a An ant is small but a hippo is _____.

b A rock is hard but cotton wool is _____.

c The sun is hot but snow is _____.

d Sugar is sweet but a lemon is _____.

e It is light in the day but it is _____ at night.

f A centimetre is a short distance but a kilometre is a _____ way.

2 Write out the following sentences, replacing each underlined word with one that means the opposite.

a The road was very <u>bendy</u>. _____

b My shorts were very <u>muddy</u>. _____

c Is my drink <u>hot</u>? _____

d Are lions <u>tame</u> animals? _____

e The sea was <u>calm</u>. _____

f I don't like <u>sweet</u> things. _____

Remember

When the letters **th** come together in a word, they make **one** sound.

To make the **th** sound, put your tongue between your front teeth and blow!

thief

Have a go

1 Complete each word with **th**. Read the words you make.

a <u>th</u>in   b clo____   c ____ing   d too____   e pa____

<u>thin</u>   _____   _____   _____   _____

f ____ick   g ____ank   h ba____   i ____ink   j bo____

_____   _____   _____   _____   _____

2 Write the words you made in this chart:

words beginning with **th**	words ending with **th**

3 Write the **th** word that rhymes with:

a wing _____   b wink _____

c moth _____   d bin _____

e bank _____   f wick _____

Unit 24: Writing *wh* words

Remember

When the letters **wh** come together in a word, they make **one** sound.

wheel   **wh**ale

Have a go

1 Complete these words. One has been done for you.

wh				
when	__at	__ich	__y	__ere
when	_____	_____	_____	_____

wh				
__eel	__ale	__ile	__ip	__isk
_____	_____	_____	_____	_____

2 Write the five **wh** words that you could use to begin a question.

_____ _____ _____ _____ _____

3 Underline a small word inside each of these words:

when	where	wheel	whale	what	whip

4 Write a **wh** word that:

a you find in the kitchen   _____

b lives in the sea   _____

c rhymes with ship   _____

d rhymes with mile   _____

e you find on a car   _____

A noun may be either **singular** or **plural**.
Singular means **one** thing. Plural means **more than one** thing.
We just **add s** to the **end** of many nouns to make them plural.

one rabbit   lots of rabbit**s**

Have a go

1 Add **s** to each singular noun to make it plural.
One has been done for you.

singular	plural
one shoe	lots of <u>shoes</u>
one book	lots of _____
one coat	lots of _____
one shirt	lots of _____
one cap	lots of _____
one dog	lots of _____

2 Rewrite each sentence correctly.

The underlined noun in each sentence is wrong.

a There were lots of <u>cow</u> in the field.   _____

b I picked up a <u>cakes</u> and ate it.   _____

c Some <u>lion</u> roar loudly.   _____

d All the <u>duck</u> were on the pond.   _____

e One <u>squirrels</u> was looking for a nut.   _____

f Lots of <u>girl</u> were riding their bikes.   _____

Unit 26: Verbs — *ing* and *ed* endings

● Remember

Sometimes a verb may end in **ing**. Sometimes a verb may end in **ed**.

The dog **is barking**.   Yesterday the dog **chased** a cat.

● Have a go

❶ Complete the verbs in this chart. Read the verbs you make.

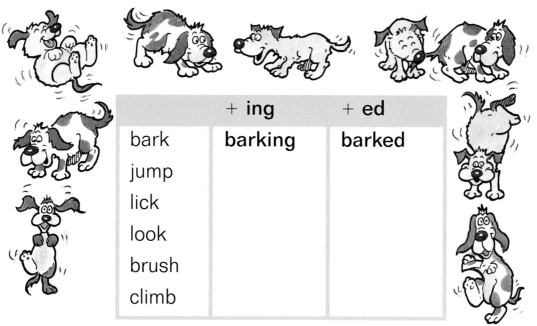

	+ ing	+ ed
bark	**barking**	**barked**
jump		
lick		
look		
brush		
climb		

❷ Now complete the verbs in these charts. Take care with your spelling!

	+ ing	+ ed
like	**liking**	**liked**
stroke		
hope		
wave		
close		
use		

	+ ing	+ ed
wag	**wagging**	**wagged**
beg		
hop		
rub		
skip		
plan		

Remember

Commas are used to **separate** things in a **list**.

mouse, hamster, gerbil, guinea pig

Have a go

1 Put in the missing commas in these lists.

a orange blue red green yellow

b horse cow goat sheep hen

c curry spaghetti pizza hamburger sausages

d guitar drums piano trumpet trombone

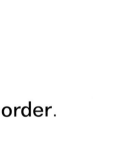

e hammer chisel saw screwdriver drill

f shirt trousers socks shorts tie

2 List the names of these animals in **alphabetical order**. Don't forget the commas!

a camel alligator deer bear

_____

b goat elephant fox horse

_____

c panda kangaroo ostrich jaguar monkey

_____

d tiger wolf rabbit yak sheep

_____

e ox hedgehog panther lion duck

_____

 **Remember**

When we want to **separate** things in a **list** we use a comma.

ant, spider, beetle, fly

 **Have a go**

Sort these words into lists. There are five words in each list.
Don't forget to put commas between each word in your lists.

| plate | Monday | apple | car | Sunday |

| pear | saucer | lorry | fox | potato |

| Tuesday | bike | cup | onion | bus |

| peach | cat | carrot | chicken | bowl |

| Thursday | cabbage | dish | duck | banana |

| van | sprout | Friday | turkey | grapes |

animals	fox, cat, chicken, duck, turkey
vegetables	
fruit	
crockery	
days of the week	
transport	

● **Remember**

When you say longer words **slowly** you can hear how they can be **broken down into smaller parts**. These parts are called **syllables**.

gar + den = garden
(two syllables)

Tap out the syllables when you say each word.

● **Have a go**

❶ Do these syllable sums. Each word has two syllables.

a car + pet = ___carpet___   b hap + py = _____

c rab + bit = _____   d mag + net = _____

e help + ful = _____   f cab + bage = _____

g sing + ing = _____   h an + gry = _____

i tur + key = _____   j ro + bot = _____

❷ Use the words with two syllables to label the pictures.

a	b	c	d	e

_____	_____	_____	_____	_____

f	g	h	i	j

_____	_____	_____	_____	_____

Remember

Words are made up of chunks of sounds or **syllables**.

gig + gle = giggle
(two syllables)

Tap out the syllables when you say each word.

Have a go

1 Break these words into syllables. Each word has two syllables.

a | tennis | **ten** | **nis**
b | football | |
c | trumpet | |
d | jumping | |
e | hundred | |
f | pencil | |
g | puddle | |
h | baby | |
i | hamster | |
j | puppy | |

2 Use the words to label the pictures.

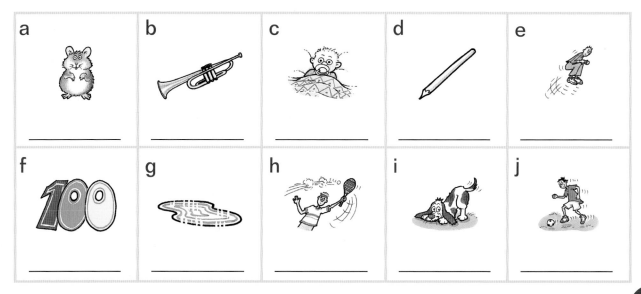

a

b

c

d

e

f

g

h

i

j

Remember

Always look carefully at words to see if you can spot any **common letter patterns**.

a h**are** with a squ**are**

a girl with f**air** h**air**

Have a go

1 Make these words. Read the words you make.

a	b	c	d
sh are	c are	s c are	s t are
__share__	_____	_____	_____

2 Write the correct word from question 1 under each picture.

a
__care__

b

_____

c
_____

d
_____

3 Complete each word with **air**. Read the words you make.

a	b	c	d
ch_____	p_____	h_____	f_____y

4 Write the correct word from question 3 under each picture.

a

_____

b

_____

c

_____

d

_____

Unit 32: Looking at *or* and *aw*

● Remember

Or and aw are **common letter patterns**.

a c**or**k and a f**or**k

a p**aw** and a s**aw**

● Have a go

Make some new words.		Change the		Write the new words. Read the new words.
a	corn	→	c to t	→	torn
b	torch	→	t to p	→	
c	port	→	p to sh	→	
d	horn	→	h to b	→	
e	form	→	f to st	→	
f	saw	→	s to j	→	
g	paw	→	p to cl	→	
h	draw	→	dr to str	→	
i	yawn	→	y to d	→	
j	crawl	→	cr to dr	→	

A **conjunction** is a **joining** word. We use a **conjunction** to join two short sentences together to make one longer sentence.

I got up. I got dressed.   I got up **and** I got dressed.

Write each pair of sentences as one long sentence.
Join them with the conjunction **and**.

a The dog barked. The cat ran away.

_____

b I picked up my book. I read it.

_____

c I dropped the ball. It bounced in the road.

_____

d Mr Shah opened the garage. He got his car out.

_____

e There are no clouds in the sky. The sun is shining.

_____

f I went to the shop. I bought some sweets.

_____

g The bird flew down. It caught a worm.

_____

h Cara has dark hair. She has brown eyes.

_____

Unit 34: Joining sentences (2)

Remember

A **conjunction** is a **joining** word.
It is used to join two short sentences
together to make one longer sentence.
Another joining word is **but**.

> Sam is tall. Emma is short.
>
> Sam is tall **but** Emma is short.

Write each pair of sentences as one long sentence.
Join them with either **and** or **but**.

a   Kate loved the heat. Emma loved the cold.

_____

b   The dog ran to the door. It barked loudly.

_____

c   The man stopped his car. He got out of it.

_____

d   A hare is fast. A snail is slow.

_____

e   Butter is soft. Iron is hard.

_____

f   My bottle is empty. Your bottle is full.

_____

g   Mrs Smith opened the door. She came in.

_____

h   Laura passed the test. Sarah failed.

_____

i   I opened my book. I began to read.

_____

j   I like apples. I don't like pears.

_____

Remember

We use an **exclamation** mark at the end of a statement or command when we **feel strongly** about something.

Stop shouting**!**

Have a go

1 Tick ☑ the sentences that end with exclamation marks.

a Get me out of here! ☐   b Where are you? ☐   c It is raining. ☐

d How nice to see you! ☐   e I love ice creams! ☐   f Did you call me? ☐

g There are six pencils. ☐   h Stop pushing me! ☐   i Can you do it? ☐

j Help! I'm stuck! ☐   k What a horrible day! ☐   l It is Saturday. ☐

2 Read each sentence. Rewrite each exclamation correctly. Put in the capital letters and exclamation marks.

a come here at once _____

b stop annoying me _____

c don't do that _____

d what a lovely picture _____

e it's not fair _____

f this is terrible _____

g what a sensible child you are _____

h be quiet _____

Unit 36: Using exclamation marks (2)

Remember

We use an **exclamation mark** to show we have strong feelings about something.

Stop pushing me!

Have a go

1 Write each exclamation under the correct picture.

This smells awful!   Ready, steady, go!   How nice to see you!

What a horrible day!   I love sweets!   Stop pulling me!

a	b	c
I love sweets!	_____	_____

d	e	f
_____	_____	_____

2 Write an exclamation in each speech bubble.

Remember

Doing words are called **verbs**.

The **past tense of a verb** tells us what someone or something has done in the past.

The rabbit hopped away.

Have a go

1 Write the correct verb in each gap.

kicked   cooked   opened   played   walked   combed

a   Yesterday I _____ the door.

b   Yesterday I _____ with my friend.

c   Yesterday I _____ to school.

d   Yesterday I _____ with a ball.

e   Yesterday I _____ my hair.

f   Yesterday I _____ an egg.

2 Fill each gap with a suitable verb.

a   Yesterday I _____ my cup of tea with a spoon.

b   Yesterday I _____ television.

c   Yesterday I _____ my teeth.

d   Yesterday I _____ some seeds in the garden.

e   Yesterday I _____ a picture with a paint brush.

f   Yesterday I _____ in bed until 9 o'clock.

Unit 38: Verbs — the past tense (2)

Remember

Sometimes the **past tense** of a verb is made of **two words**.

The boy **was eating** an apple.

Have a go

1 Choose 'was' or 'were' to complete each sentence.

a   The sun _____ shining.

b   The birds _____ singing.

c   I _____ running.

d   We _____ eating ice creams.

e   The children _____ shouting.

f   The girl _____ crying.

g   The lions _____ roaring.

h   The snake _____ hissing.

2 Write each sentence again. Use two words for each verb.

a   The camel <u>walked</u> slowly.   **The camel was walking slowly.**

b   The children <u>laughed</u> loudly.   _____

c   The train <u>stopped</u> at the station.   _____

d   The lorries <u>travelled</u> up the motorway.   _____

e   I <u>baked</u> a cake.   _____

f   Our teacher <u>helped</u> us.   _____

Remember

Sometimes we use **speech bubbles** to show someone is speaking. The **words the person says** go **inside** the speech bubbles.

What's for dinner?

You can have fish fingers or pizza.

Have a go

I like books.

Vicky

I like to play.

Rehannah

I like my trainers.

Jack

I like cats.

Claire

I like my computer games.

Alex

I like playing football.

Toby

Write what each of these children said:

a Alex: _____

b Vicky: _____

c Jack: _____

d Toby: _____

e Rehannah: _____

f Claire: _____

Unit 40: Speech (2)

● Remember

In pictures we use **speech bubbles** to show someone is speaking. The **words the person says** go **inside** the speech bubbles.

When we write, we use **speech marks** to show when someone is **speaking**. We write what the person says **inside** the speech marks.

Ben said, "I like crisps."

● Have a go

Write what each person said inside the correct speech marks.

a   The baker said, "_____"

b   The doctor said, "_____"

c   The dentist said, "_____"

d   The policewoman said, "_____"

e   The shop assistant said, "_____"

f   The builder said, "_____"

g   The footballer said, "_____"

Check how much you have learned.

Answer the questions.
Mark your answers. Fill in your score.

SCORE

1 Fill in the missing vowel in each word.

a    b

c___t   d___ck

out of 2

2 Do these word sums. Write the words you make.

out of 2

a p + e + n = ____   b h + o + t = ____

3 Underline the two words that rhyme.

out of 2

 pin   ten   win

4 Circle the best ending for each sentence.

a flower.

a The girl climbed

a tree.

a balloon.

out of 2

b The boy popped

a bat.

5 Write these sentences correctly.

a it rained a lot

_____

b we got very wet

_____

out of 2

6 Fill each gap with the correct noun.

clock   book

out of 2

a You read a _____.

b A _____ tells us the time.

7 Write the words in the correct order in each sentence.

out of 2

a A barks dog.   _____

b A likes milk cat.   _____

8 Choose the correct word.

out of 2

a You _____ (part, park) a car.

b At night it is _____ (dark, dart).

9 Make some compound words.

out of 2

a foot + ball = _____

b moon + light = _____

out of 2

10 Fill each gap with a suitable verb.

a You d_____ a car.

b You p_____ a flower.

Total out of 20

Check how much you have learned.

Answer the questions.
Mark your answers. Fill in your score.

SCORE

1 Write the opposite of:

a empty _____   b heavy _____

out of 2

2 Choose the correct word for each picture.

a   b

| bath | path |
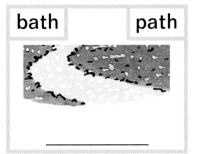
_____

| moth | cloth |
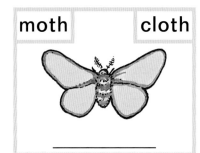
_____

out of 2

3 Fill in the missing words.

singular	plural
a one sock	two _____
b one shoe	two _____

out of 2

4 Put in the missing commas.

a black blue white yellow

b tree flower bush shrub

out of 2

5 Do these syllable sums:

a ta + ble = _____   b set + tee = _____

out of 2

6 Choose **are** or **air** to fill each gap.

a ch_____   b squ_____

7 Write each pair of sentences as one long sentence.
Join them with the conjunction **and**.

a It is raining. It is cold.

_____

b I went home. I had my tea.

_____

8 Write each exclamation correctly.

a it isn't fair   _____

b this is wonderful   _____

9 Think of a sensible verb to complete these sentences.

a Yesterday I _____ a song.

b Yesterday I _____ football.

10 Write each sentence in the correct speech bubble.

I make bread.   I mend cars.

a   b

Check how much you have learned.

Answer the questions.
Mark your answers. Fill in your score.

SCORE

❶ Fill in the missing vowels.

a
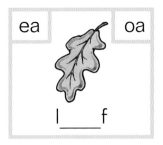

| ea | | oa |

l___f

b
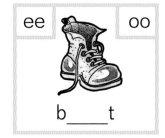

| ee | | oo |

b___t

out of 2

❷ Add the phonemes. Make the words.

a   **g** + **r** + **ow** = _____

b   **sh** + **ee** + **p** = _____

out of 2

❸ Underline the pair of words that rhyme.

book   good   look

out of 2

❹ Cross out the word that is not needed in each sentence.

a The girl ran climbed a tree.

b A ball is under on the tree.

out of 2

❺ Write these questions correctly.

a   what is the time   _____

b   where are you going   _____

out of 2

6 Write **a** or **an** in each gap.

a

___ egg

b

___ spoon

7 Rewrite each sentence so it makes sense.

a The egg fried the woman.

_____

b You hit a hammer with a nail.

_____

8 Choose **oi** or **oy** to fill each gap.

a

b____

b

b____l

9 Write the two words that make up each compound word.

a _____ + _____ = bookcase

b _____ + _____ = hairbrush

10 Choose **is** or **are** to complete each sentence.

a It _____ sunny.

b We _____ getting very hot.

Check how much you have learned.

Answer the questions.
Mark your answers. Fill in your score.

SCORE

1 Write the opposite of:

a hard _____

b heavy _____

out of 2

2 Choose the correct word for each sentence.

a A _____ (wheel, while) is round.

out of 2

b A _____ (while, whale) lives in the sea.

3 Write each verb correctly.

a hopeing _____

b rubing _____

out of 2

4 Put in the missing commas.

a **duck goat horse cow**

b **cup saucer plate dish**

out of 2

5 Work out these syllable sums.

a car + pet = _____

b kit + ten = _____

out of 2

6 Choose the correct letter pattern.

a
| or | | aw |

s_____

b
| or | | aw |

t_____ch

out of 2

7 Write each pair of sentences as one long sentence. Join them with either **and** or **but**.

a I like potatoes. I don't like cabbage.

_____

b I sat down. I watched TV.

_____

out of 2

8 Write each exclamation correctly.

a stop pushing me _____

b what a horrid smell _____

out of 2

9 Choose 'was' or 'were' to complete the sentence.

a Lots of fish _____ swimming in the water.

b She _____ riding her bicycle.

out of 2

10 Write what each person said.

I do magic tricks.

I grow flowers.

a The magician said, "_____"

b The gardener said, "_____"

out of 2

Total out of 20

Parents' notes

Units 1 and 2: Vowels and consonants   The letters of the alphabet may be divided into vowels and consonants. There are five vowels – **a**, **e**, **i**, **o** and **u**. All the other letters are consonants. Every word must have at least one vowel in it. (Note that the letter **y** sometimes acts as a part-time vowel in words like 'my'.)

Units 3 and 4: Word-building with phonemes   All words are made up of phonemes (units of sound). Sometimes phonemes may be single letters. Sometimes they consist of two or more letters which make one sound e.g. **ea**. Your child needs to know how to build up words using phonemes.

Units 5 and 6: Rhyming   Rhyming involves good listening skills. The ability to differentiate and hear differences in sounds and rhymes is an important early reading and spelling skill. In these units the rhyming parts of the pairs of words sound and look similar.

Units 7 and 8: Writing sensible sentences and Looking carefully at sentences   Remind your child that all sentences they read or write should make sense. Remind your child to check sentences he or she has written to make sure they make sense. It is easy to add extra words or leave words out.

Unit 9: Capital letters and full stops   All sentences should begin with a capital letter. Most sentences end with a full stop. (Note that questions and exclamations do not.) The full stop is an important sign to the reader. It helps break up the text into meaningful units, and it indicates when to take a pause.

Unit 10: Question marks and full stops   All sentences should begin with a capital letter. Most sentences end with a full stop. However, when a question is being asked, the sentence must end with a question mark.

Unit 11: Checking up on nouns   All words may be classified according to the jobs they do in sentences. Nouns (naming words) play an essential part in grammar.

Unit 12: Nouns – *a* or *an*?   It is important for your child to recognise that when a noun begins with a consonant the indefinite article **a** is used. When the noun begins with a vowel the indefinite article **an** is used.

Units 13 and 14: Sentences and Silly sentences   We make sentences by putting words in order. The order we arrange the words in can make a lot of difference! It is always a good idea to get your child to read through a finished piece of work to check that each sentence he or she has written makes sense.

Unit 15: The *ar* letter pattern   There are many common letter patterns (letters which frequently come together) in words. It is important for your child to recognise these when reading and to be able to use them when writing. The letter pattern **ar** is the focus of this unit.

Unit 16: Letter patterns – *oi* and *oy*   The letter patterns **oi** and **oy** (which both sound the same) are the focus of this unit. Point out that **oy** usually comes at the end of a word, whereas **oi** usually comes within a word.

Units 17 and 18: Making compound words   Compound words are words that are made by joining two smaller words together to make one longer word. A useful spelling strategy to learn is to look for smaller words 'hiding' inside longer words.

Units 19 and 20: Revising verbs   All words may be classified according to the jobs they do in sentences. Verbs (doing words) play an essential part in grammar.

Units 21 and 22: Opposite meanings   Antonyms are words whose meanings are as different as possible from each other i.e. opposites.

Unit 23: Spelling and writing *th* words   The phoneme **th** is the focus of this unit. Whenever the letters **th** come together your child needs to know that they are not sounded separately, but make one sound.

Unit 24: Writing *wh* words   The phoneme **wh** is the focus of this unit. Whenever the letters **wh** come together your child needs to know that they are not sounded separately, but make one sound. Many questions begin with **wh** words e.g. why, where, when, what, which.

Unit 25: Singular and plural   Remind your child that many words may be extended by adding suffixes (word endings). In this unit turning single nouns into their plural form by adding **s** is studied (e.g. one car but two car**s**).

Unit 26: Verbs – *ing* and *ed* endings   Remind your child that many words may be extended by adding suffixes (word endings). In this unit the common verb endings **ing** and **ed** are the focus.

Units 27 and 28: Using commas in lists   We use commas to separate items in a list. Commas are a signal to the reader to pause briefly.

Units 29 and 30: Understanding syllables   When we say words slowly we can hear how they may be broken down into smaller parts, called syllables. It is helpful to tap or clap these 'beats' when saying words to stress the syllables. Another way is to get your child to say the words like a robot or Dalek!

Unit 31: Looking at *are* and *air*   It is important to get your child to look carefully at groups of words to try to spot any common letter patterns (letters which frequently come together) in them. These are often important as 'building blocks' for reading and writing. The letter patterns **are** (as in 'square') and **air** (as in 'chair') are the focus of this unit.

Unit 32: Looking at *or* and *aw*   It is important to get your child to look carefully at groups of words to try to spot any common letter patterns (letters which frequently come together) in them. These are often important as 'building blocks' for reading and writing. The letter patterns **or** and **aw** (which both sound the same!) are the focus of this unit.

Units 33 and 34: Joining sentences   A conjunction is a joining word which may be used to join two sentences together. Two common conjunctions are the words **and** and **but**. In order to understand this idea, it is helpful to get your child to think of a road junction where two roads meet.

Units 35 and 36: Using exclamation marks   An exclamation mark is a signal to the reader. An exclamation mark is used at the end of a sentence to show strong feelings about something.

Units 37 and 38: Verbs – the past tense   The **past tense** of verbs (doing words) tell us what someone or something did in the past. Sometimes we use just one word e.g. 'The girl **shouted** loudly.' Sometimes we may use two words to express the past tense e.g. 'The girl was **shouting** loudly'.

Units 39 and 40: Speech   Your child will be familiar with the concept of speech bubbles through picture books and comics. Remind your child that all the words the person actually says go inside the speech bubble itself. When writing, all the words the person says go inside speech marks.

Answers

Unit 1: Vowels and consonants (1) (page 4)

1 h<u>a</u>t, b<u>e</u>d, p<u>i</u>n, c<u>o</u>t, b<u>u</u>t, s<u>i</u>p, f<u>a</u>t, s<u>u</u>n, g<u>e</u>t, p<u>o</u>t, h<u>u</u>g, n<u>e</u>t, l<u>a</u>p, f<u>o</u>g, b<u>i</u>n.

2 a frog   b drum   c sack   d leg
e kiss   f rug   g hill   h nest
i map   j bag

Unit 2: Vowels and consonants (2) (page 5)

1 a fan   b net   c zip   d rod   e jug
f bell   g duck   h king   i wall   j clock

2 a tree   b bike   c loaf   d boat
e moon   f rain   g cube   h sweet
i road   j glue

Unit 3: Word-building with phonemes (1) (page 6)

1 a map   b hen   c six   d cot   e hut
f zip   g peg   h cap   i log   j mug

2 a cot   b map   c hut   d six   e hen
f zip   g log   h cap   i peg   j mug

Unit 4: Word-building with phonemes (2) (page 7)

a frog   b deer
c goat   d rat
e chick   f snail
g snake   h duck
i fox   j sheep

Ensure your child can match each word to the correct animal.

Unit 5: Rhyming (1) (page 8)

stay	tray	lost	cost
hill	fill	meet	greet
lick	stick	bite	white
slow	throw	moan	groan
cry	try	rain	drain

Unit 6: Rhyming (2) (page 9)

1 Ensure your child has coloured each balloon correctly.

2

ight words	ook words	ound words	ark words
bright	book	bound	bark
fight	cook	found	dark
light	crook	ground	lark
might	look	round	mark
night	shook	sound	park

Unit 7: Writing sensible sentences (page 10)

a A car has four wheels.
b The mouse squeaked.
c Tom drank a cup of tea.
d The girl read the book.
e A squirrel ran up the tree.
f An apple has lots of pips.
g The lion roared.

Unit 8: Looking carefully at sentences (page 11)

1 a The cat sat on the mat.
b A house has a roof.
c The boy read a book.
d I fell into the water.
e The girl lost her bag.
f The plane flew in the sky.

2 The answers below are examples only. Other answers are possible.

a cold   b round   c sour
d kitten   e boil   f hit

Unit 9: Capital letters and full stops (page 12)

a Claire ran home from school.
b She felt very hungry.
c Claire went into the kitchen.
d She made some cheese sandwiches.
e Then she put some cakes on the table.
f Next Claire put some crisps in a dish.
g After this she made a drink.
h When everything was ready Claire had her tea.

Unit 10: Question marks and full stops (page 13)

a When is your birthday?
  It is in September.
b Where do you live?
  I live in Bedford.
c What do you like at school?
  I like reading best.
d What is the capital of France?
  Paris is the capital of France.
e Which is the first month of the year?
  January is the first month.
f In which month is Christmas?
  Christmas is in December.

Unit 11: Checking up on nouns (page 14)

1 a boat b ambulance c aeroplane
    d fire engine e submarine f train

2 a school   b hammer   c tap
    d money   e knife   f window

Unit 12: Nouns – *a* or *an*? (page 15)

1 a **an** ant   b **a** hat   c **a** cap
    d **an** egg   e **a** ladder
    f **an** umbrella   g **an** ostrich
    h **a** sock

2 a I saw **an** ostrich eating **an** orange.
    b Sam had **a** drink from **a** bottle.
    c You will need **an** umbrella in **a** rainstorm.
    d **A** child sat on **an** ant.
    e Will you buy me **a** comic from **a** shop?
    f There was **an** aeroplane on the runway at **an** airport.

Unit 13: Sentences (page 16)

1 Sharks swim.   Horses gallop.
    Snakes slither.   Frogs hop.
    Birds fly.   Butterflies flutter.

2 You drink a cup of tea.
    The butterfly fluttered its wings.
    My shorts are very muddy.
    You drive a car on the road.
    An astronaut flies in a rocket.
    Dogs like to eat bones.

Unit 14: Silly sentences (page 17)

1
a The boy ate the egg.
b The lady cooked the cake.
c The man drove the car.
d The squirrel ran up the tree.
e The shark ate the fish.
f The girl picked up the case.
g The monkey peeled a banana.
h The teacher read a book.

2 Answers will vary.

Unit 15: The *ar* letter pattern (page 18)

1
a car   b bar   c far   d jar
e tar   f star

2 d<u>ar</u>k, h<u>ar</u>m, p<u>ar</u>t, sh<u>ar</u>k, ch<u>ar</u>m, p<u>ar</u>ty, sm<u>ar</u>t, f<u>ar</u>m, sp<u>ar</u>k, b<u>ar</u>k, ch<u>ar</u>t, al<u>ar</u>m, p<u>ar</u>k, c<u>ar</u>t, l<u>ar</u>k, d<u>ar</u>t

3

arm words	**ark** words	**art** words
harm	dark	part
charm	shark	party
farm	spark	smart
alarm	bark	chart
	park	cart
	lark	dart

Unit 16: Letter patterns – *oi* and *oy* (page 19)

1 a coil   b point   c joy   d toy

2 a point   b toy   c coil   d joy

3 a boy   b joint   c coin   d enjoy
e annoy/spoil

Unit 17: Compound words (1) (page 20)

1
a farmyard   b seaside
c bathroom   d sheepdog
e sunshine   f snowman
g keyhole   h runway

2
a seaside   b keyhole
c snowman   d runway
e farmyard   f bathroom
g sheepdog   h sunshine

Unit 18: Compound words (2) (page 21)

football   hairbrush
bedroom   butterfly
bookcase   sunshine
windmill   handbag
motorway   tablecloth
grandmother

Unit 19: Revising verbs (1) (page 22)

1 a read   b sing   c tie   d comb
e eat   f bang

2 a climb   b paint   c ride   d mow
e catch   f sleep

Unit 20: Revising verbs (2) (page 23)

1 a is   b are   c are   d is   e are
f is   g are   h is

2
a Mr Smith is washing his car.
b The teacher is helping Sam.
c Beth is painting a lovely picture.
d The cat is drinking some milk.
e The lady is picking up her bag.
f A farmer is working on his farm.

Unit 21: Opposite meanings (1) (page 24)

sad	happy	near	far
fast	slow	noisy	quiet
hot	cold	open	shut
wet	dry	weak	strong
long	short	fat	thin
heavy	light		

Unit 22: Opposite meanings (2) (page 25)

1 a huge   b soft   c cold   d sour
e dark   f long

2 The answers below are examples.
Other answers are possible.
a straight   b clean   c cold
d wild   e rough   f sour

Unit 23: Spelling and writing *th* words (page 26)

1 a thin   b cloth   c thing   d tooth
e path   f thick   g thank   h bath
i think   j both

2

words beginning with **th**	words ending with **th**
thin	cloth
thing	tooth
thick	path
thank	bath
think	both

3 a thing   b think   c cloth   d thin
e thank   f thick

Unit 24: Writing *wh* words (page 27)

1 when   what   which   why   where
wheel   whale   while   whip   whisk

2 when   what   which   why   where

3 hen   here   heel   hale/ale
hat   hip

4 a whisk   b whale   c whip
d while   e wheel

Unit 25: Singular and plural (page 28)

1

singular	plural
one shoe	lots of shoes
one book	lots of books
one coat	lots of coats
one shirt	lots of shirts
one cap	lots of caps
one dog	lots of dogs

2 a There were lots of cows in the field.

b I picked up a cake and ate it.

c Some lions roar loudly.

d All the ducks were on the pond.

e One squirrel was looking for a nut.

f Lots of girls were riding their bikes.

Unit 26: Verbs – *ing* and *ed* endings (page 29)

1

	+ ing	+ ed
bark	barking	barked
jump	jumping	jumped
lick	licking	licked
look	looking	looked
brush	brushing	brushed
climb	climbing	climbed

2

	+ ing	+ ed
like	liking	liked
stroke	stroking	stroked
hope	hoping	hoped
wave	waving	waved
close	closing	closed
use	using	used

	+ ing	+ ed
wag	wagging	wagged
beg	begging	begged
hop	hopping	hopped
rub	rubbing	rubbed
skip	skipping	skipped
plan	planning	planned

Unit 27: Using commas in lists (1) (page 30)

1
a orange, blue, red, green, yellow
b horse, cow, goat, sheep, hen
c curry, spaghetti, pizza, hamburger, sausages
d guitar, drums, piano, trumpet, trombone
e hammer, chisel, saw, screwdriver, drill
f shirt, trousers, socks, shorts, tie

2
a alligator, bear, camel, deer
b elephant, fox, goat, horse
c jaguar, kangaroo, monkey, ostrich, panda
d rabbit, sheep, tiger, wolf, yak
e duck, hedgehog, lion, ox, panther

Unit 28: Using commas in lists (2) (page 31)

animals	fox, cat, chicken, duck, turkey
vegetables	potato, onion, carrot, cabbage, sprout
fruit	apple, pear, peach, banana, grapes
crockery	plate, saucer, cup, bowl, dish
days of the week	Monday, Sunday, Tuesday, Thursday, Friday
transport	car, lorry, bike, bus, van

Unit 29: Understanding syllables (1) (page 32)

1 a carpet   b happy   c rabbit
d magnet   e helpful   f cabbage
g singing   h angry   i turkey
j robot

2 a magnet   b rabbit   c robot
d carpet   e singing   f cabbage
g angry   h turkey   i happy
j helpful

Unit 30: Understanding syllables (2) (page 33)

1 a ten/nis   b foot/ball   c trum/pet
d jump/ing   e hun/dred   f pen/cil
g pud/dle   h ba/by   i ham/ster
j pup/py

2 a hamster   b trumpet   c baby
d pencil   e jumping   f hundred
g puddle   h tennis   i puppy
j football

Unit 31: Looking at *are* and *air* (page 34)

1 a share b care c scare d stare

2 a care b share c stare d scare

3 a chair b pair c hair d fairy

4 a hair b chair c fairy d pair

Unit 32: Looking at *or* and *aw* (page 35)

a torn b porch c short d born
e storm f jaw g claw h straw
i dawn j drawl

Unit 33: Joining sentences (1) (page 36)

a The dog barked **and** the cat ran away.

b I picked up my book **and** I read it.

c I dropped the ball **and** it bounced in the road.

d Mr Shah opened the garage **and** he got his car out.

e There are no clouds in the sky **and** the sun is shining.

f I went to the shop **and** I bought some sweets.

g The bird flew down **and** it caught a worm.

h Cara has dark hair **and** she has brown eyes.

Unit 34: Joining sentences (2) (page 37)

a Kate loved the heat **but** Emma loved the cold.

b The dog ran to the door **and** it barked loudly.

c The man stopped his car **and** he got out of it.

d A hare is fast **but** a snail is slow.

e Butter is soft **but** iron is hard.

f My bottle is empty **but** your bottle is full.

g Mrs Smith opened the door **and** she came in.

h Laura passed the test **but** Sarah failed.

i I opened my book **and** I began to read.

j I like apples **but** I don't like pears.

Unit 35: Using exclamation marks (1) (page 38)

1 a Get me out of here! √
 b Where are you?
 c It is raining.
 d How nice to see you! √
 e I love ice creams! √
 f Did you call me?
 g There are six pencils.
 h Stop pushing me! √
 i Can you do it?
 j Help! I'm stuck! √
 k What a horrible day! √
 l It is Saturday.

②
a Come here at once!
b Stop annoying me!
c Don't do that!
d What a lovely picture!
e It's not fair!
f This is terrible!
g What a sensible child you are!
h Be quiet!

Unit 36: Exclamation marks (2) (page 39)

①
a I love sweets!
b This smells awful!
c Ready, steady, go!
d What a horrible day!
e Stop pulling me!
f How nice to see you!

② Answers will vary. Make sure your child has used the exclamation mark correctly.

Unit 37: Past tense (1) (page 40)

①
a opened   b played
c walked   d kicked
e combed   f cooked

②
a stirred   b watched
c brushed   d planted
e painted   f stayed

Unit 38: Past tense (2) (page 41)

①
a was   b were
c was   d were
e were   f was
g were   h was

②
a The camel was walking slowly.
b The children were laughing loudly.
c The train was stopping at the station.
d The lorries were travelling up the motorway.
e I was baking a cake.
f Our teacher was helping us.

Unit 39: Speech (1) (page 42)

a Alex: I like my computer games.
b Vicky: I like books.
c Jack: I like my trainers.
d Toby: I like playing football.
e Rehannah: I like to play.
f Claire: I like cats.

Unit 40: Speech (2) (page 43)

a The baker said, "I make bread and cakes."
b The doctor said, "You have got the measles."
c The dentist said, "Open wide, please."
d The policewoman said, "It is safe to cross the road now."
e The shop assistant said, "May I help you?"
f The builder said, "I build houses."
g The footballer said, "I scored two goals."

Test 1 (pages 44 and 45)

1 a cat   b duck

2 a pen   b hot

3 pin   win

4 a The girl climbed a tree.
    b The boy popped a balloon.

5 a It rained a lot.
    b We got very wet.

6 a book   b clock

7 a A dog barks.   b A cat likes milk.

8 a park   b dark

9 a football   b moonlight

10 a drive   b pick/plant

Test 2 (pages 46 and 47)

1 a full   b light

2 a path   b moth

3 a socks   b shoes

4 a black, blue, white, yellow
    b tree, flower, bush, shrub

5 a table   b settee

6 a chair   b square

7 a It is raining and it is cold.
    b I went home and I had my tea.

8 a It isn't fair!   b This is wonderful!

9 a sang   b played

10 a I mend cars.   b I make bread.

Test 3 (pages 48 and 49)

1 a leaf   b b**oo**t

2 a grow   b sheep

3 <u>book</u> <u>look</u>

4 a The girl ~~ran~~ climbed a tree.
b A ball is under ~~on~~ the tree.

5 a What is the time?
b Where are you going?

6 a **an** egg   b **a** spoon

7 a The woman fried the egg.
b You hit a nail with a hammer.

8 a b**oy**   b b**oi**l

9 a book + case   b hair + brush

10 a is   b are

Test 4 (pages 50 and 51)

1 a soft/easy   b light

2 a wheel   b whale

3 a hoping   b rubbing

4 a duck, goat, horse, cow
b cup, saucer, plate, dish

5 a carpet   b kitten

6 a saw   b torch

7 a I like potatoes **but** I don't like cabbage.
b I sat down **and** I watched TV.

8 a Stop pushing me!
b What a horrid smell!

9 a were   b was

10 a The magician said, "I do magic tricks."
b The gardener said, "I grow flowers."